Twist and Jump

Written by Clare Helen Welsh
Illustrated by Sylwia Filipczak

Collins

sprint on the spot

the coach stands still

sprint on the spot

the coach stands still

spring up and grab it

a long black vest

spring up and grab it

a long black vest

a swift jump

her hand blocks the shot

a swift jump

her hand blocks the shot

a strong jump

she twists and skids to a stop

a strong jump

she twists and skids to a stop

the shot slips into the hoop

they stand and clap

the shot slips into the hoop

they stand and clap

Review: After reading

Use your assessment from hearing the children read to choose any GPCs, words or tricky words that need additional practice.

Read 1: Decoding
- Turn to page 6. Point to **spring** and model sounding out (*s/p/r/i/ng*), then blending to read the whole word. (*spring*)
- Ask the children to read these words, sounding out then blending:

  spot   **black**   **swift**   **jump**
- Say: Can you blend in your head silently when you read these words aloud?
- Turn to page 15. Point to **stop** for the children to read. Check that they blend "s" and "t" smoothly. On page 19, repeat for **stand**. Check they don't miss any of the consonants.

Read 2: Vocabulary
- Look back through the book and discuss the pictures. Encourage the children to talk about details that stand out for them. Use a dialogic talk model to expand on their ideas and recast them in full sentences as naturally as possible.
- Work together to expand vocabulary by naming objects in the pictures that children do not know.
- Discuss the meaning of **sprint on the spot** on page 2. Say: The girls are sprinting on the spot, not just jogging or running, to warm up. Ask: What words could the author have used instead of sprint? (e.g. *run very fast*)

Read 3: Comprehension
- Ask the children what they already know about basketball or other sports. Encourage them to describe their favourite sport or sports players.
- Reread page 3 and discuss what the coach is doing. (e.g. *timing the players and helping them to practise*) Turn to pages 6 and 7 and discuss why practising might be important. Then turn to pages 18 and 19 and ask: How do you think the team feels? Talk about how hard work leads to a win for the basketball team.
- Model discussing what basketball players in the book do to practise and win, using the pictures on pages 22 and 23 as prompts. Together, come up with verbs to match each picture. (e.g. *sprint, spring up, block, jump, slips in*)